Centipede

Karen Hartley,
Chris Macro
and Philip Taylor

Heinemann Library
Des Plaines, Illinois

Published by Heinemann Library,
an imprint of Reed Educational & Professional Publishing,
1350 East Touhy Avenue, Suite 240 West
Des Plaines, IL 60018

Text and cover designed by Celia Floyd
Printed and bound in Hong Kong/China by South China Printing Co. Ltd.

03 02 01 00 99
10 9 8 7 6 5 4 3 2 1

Library of Congress Cataloging-in-Publication Data
Hartley, Karen, 1949-
     Centipede / Karen Hartley, Chris Macro, and Philip Taylor.
          p. cm. – (Bug books)
     Includes bibliographical references and index.
Summary: A simple introduction to the physical characteristics,
   diet, life cycle, predators, habitat, and lifespan of centipedes.
          ISBN 1-57572-796-X (lib.bdg.)
          1. Centipedes—Juvenile literature. [1. Centipedes.] I. Macro,
Chris, 1940- . II. Taylor, Philip, 1949- . II.I Title.
   IV Series.
QL449.5.H28   1999
595.6'2—dc21
                                                    98-42671
                                                    CIP
                                                    AC

Acknowledgments
The Publishers would like to thank the following for permission to reproduce photographs:
Animals Animals/Z. Leszczynski, p. 13; R. Mendez, p.16; P. Parkes p. 26; Ardea/J. Daniels, pp.17, 24; A. Warren, p.19; Bruce Coleman Ltd./I. Arndt, p. 21; G. Cubitt, p. 8; C. and D. Frith, p.10; A. Purcell, p.14; Dr. F. Sauer, p. 4; Garden and Wildlife Matters, pp. 5, 18, 23, 29; D. Clyne/Mantis Wildlife Films, p. 6; J. Cooke, p. 25; NHPA/R. Fotheringham, p. 22; Okapia/O. Cabrero and I. Roura, p.15; U. Gross, p12; M. Kage, p. 20; Oxford Scientific Films/H. Abipp, p. 11; G. Bernard, pp. 7, 9, 27, 28.

Cover photos: Gareth Boden, (child); Bruce Coleman Ltd/K. Taylor, (centipede).

Illustration: Pennant Illustration/Alan Fraser, p. 30.

Note to the Reader

Some words are shown in bold, **like this.** You can find out
what they mean by looking in the glossary.

Contents

What Are Centipedes?

Centipedes are small animals. They have many legs. But they have no backbones. Animals without backbones are invertebrates. Centipedes have **jointed** bodies, **feelers,** and legs.

There are about 2,800 different kinds of centipedes in the world. They live in most countries. Have you seen any?

What Centipedes Look Like

Centipedes look like worms. But their heads have a **pair** of **feelers** and big jaws for biting. Just behind their heads, they have a pair of **poison fangs**.

Centipedes' bodies are thin. They may be dark, reddish, or light brown. Their bodies are made of a line of rings, called **segments**. Each segment has a pair of legs. Count the legs on this one.

How Big Are Centipedes?

Centipedes come in all sizes. The bigger they are, the more legs they have. The smaller centipedes will have at least 15 **pairs.** Bigger ones can have 170 pairs.

Some centipedes are shorter than your little finger. The giant desert centipede lives in Arizona. It can be as long as a loaf of bread.

How Centipedes Are Born

In spring, **male** and **female** centipedes **mate**. The female lays eggs. The soil centipede lays 30 to 40 eggs in a small hole. See how she wraps her body around them? This keeps them safe.

A female stone centipede lays one egg at a time. She rolls each egg in soil. The soil sticks to the eggs. This helps hide the eggs from **predators**.

How Centipedes Grow?

When the eggs **hatch,** the centipedes are tiny. They only have six or seven **pairs** of legs. But they grow quickly. They grow right out of their skin.

They **molt** by wriggling out of their old skins. A new skin grows and replaces the old one. The new skin has more **segments** and some new pairs of legs.

What Centipedes Eat

Centipedes are called **predators** because they hunt animals for food. They use their **poison fangs** to kill worms, spiders, and some **insects.**

Some types of centipedes eat fruit or potatoes. Other types eat their own babies. Animals that eat their own kind are called *cannibals*.

Which Animals Eat Centipedes?

Small **nocturnal** creatures like shrews and large beetles hunt centipedes. Some birds like to eat centipedes, too.

Blackbirds that are pecking the ground or digging with their beaks are looking for food. Maybe this one will find a centipede to eat.

Where Centipedes Live

Centipedes live under stones. They live under sheds. They live in piles of leaves or rotting logs. Others live in the soil. For them, dark, wet places are best.

Centipedes need to live where it is **damp.** They need to stay out of the sun. The biggest centipedes live in hot places, like the rainforests in South America.

How Centipedes Move

Centipedes' bodies are **jointed.** Each **segment** can bend. Being jointed helps them move. Those that live in the ground can wriggle into tiny cracks.

Some centipedes can move very quickly.
Their back legs are often bigger than
their other legs. They use these legs to
push themselves forward.

How Long Centipedes Live

No one knows how long centipedes live in the wild. Scientists who watch centipedes in a **laboratory** have kept them alive for more than five years.

Some centipedes hibernate during winter. It is colder and food is harder to find. To stay alive, centipedes go underground and sleep.

What Centipedes Do

Most centipedes help gardeners. They eat many of the **pests** that harm plants. They may bite the gardner. But most bites are not harmful to people.

Centipedes are **nocturnal** animals.
They hunt at night. They rest during the
day. They need to stay out of the sun.
The sun dries up their skin.

Centipede means 100 legs. *Centi* means 100. *Pede* means feet. It is said that they got their name because people thought that's how many legs they had!

Some kinds of centipedes have no eyes. They can feel **vibrations** made by moving animals. They use their **feelers.** Their feelers help them smell and taste.

Thinking About Centipedes

Remember that some centipedes cannot see. How do you think that they find their way around?

What do you think would happen
to a centipede on a hot summer day?
Where do centipedes like to live? How
do they help gardeners?

Bug Map

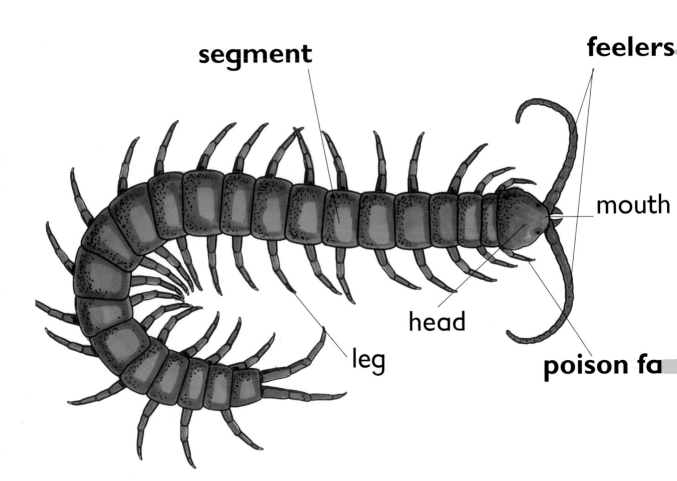

segment

feelers

mouth

head

leg

poison fa

Glossary

cannibal animal that eats its own kind

damp a little bit wet

feeler part on an animal's body for sensing touch

female woman or girl

hatch to come out of an egg

insect small animal with six legs, a body with three parts, and usually having wings

joint place where parts are joined and that helps the body move

laboratory place where scientists work

male man or boy

mate to join with another to make babies

molt to shed skin

nocturnal active at night

pair two things that are alike and belong together

pest animal that causes trouble

poison fangs teethlike body parts used for fighting

predator animal that hunts other animals

segment piece or a part of something

vibration fast shaking caused by something moving

More Books to Read

Cooper, Jason. *Centipedes.* Vero Beach, Fla: Rourke Publications, Incorporated. 1996.

Ryden, Hope. *ABC of Crawlers and Flyers.* New York: Houghton Mifflin, 1996.

Index